C# PROGRAMMING:

UPDATED FOR .NET FRAMEWORK 4.5 AND VISUAL STUDIO 2013

BECOME AN EXPERT

By Daniel Perkins

Table of Contents

Disclaimer

While all attempts have been made to verify the information provided in this book, the author does assume any responsibility for errors, omissions, or contrary interpretations of the subject matter contained within. **The information provided in this book is for educational and entertainment purposes only. The reader is responsible for his or her own actions and the author does not accept any responsibilities for any liabilities or damages, real or perceived, resulting from the use of this information.**

Introduction

C# is a very interesting programming language for programmers. The language has been widely used by developers of very useful applications of different types and the language is known for its simplicity. If you are competent in using C, C++ or Java programming languages, or you have some knowledge about them, then it will be easy for you to learn C#. Most of the constructs in these languages are closely related in terms of their syntax. After reading this book, you will be an expert in C# and be in a position to create your own C# application.

Chapter 1 - Definition

C# is a modern, object-oriented programming language which was developed by Microsoft and it was approved by the ISO (International Standards Organization) and the ECMA (European Computer Manufacturers Association). The programming language was developed during the development of the .Net Framework by Anders Hejlsberg and he developed it for CLI (Common Language Infrastructure). The CLI is made up of the runtime environment and an executable code which permits programmers to use high-level programming languages on different platforms and architectures.

The language is popular to use professionally for the following reasons:

- The programming language is modern and general purpose
- It is an object oriented programming language
- The language is component oriented
- It is easy to learn the language
- The language is a structured one

- Programs written in this programming language are very efficient
- Compilation of code written using this programming language can be done on a variety of platforms
- It is a component of the ".*Net Framework*"

The language supports numerous programming paradigms including imperative, functional, component-oriented and object-oriented programming paradigms. The language was developed to provide programmers with a mechanism to easily develop and deploy applications which can be deployed in a distributed system. The language greatly resembles Java, C and C++, those who are familiar with these programming languages will find it easy to learn C#.

The language has the following significant features:

- Integration with Windows

- Automatic Garbage Collection

- Assembly Versioning

- Boolean Conditions

- Lambda and LINQ Expressions

- Properties and Events

- Standard Library

- Events and Delegates Management

- Easy-to-use Generics

- Conditional Compilation

- Simple Multithreading

- Indexers

Chapter 2 - Setting up the Environment

We need to discuss the tools which are necessary for one to program in C#. In the previous chapter we said that C# is a component of the "*.Net Framework*", this is why the language is mostly used for development of "*.Net*" applications. However, it is good for you to understand the relationship between C# and the "*.Net Framework*" in more detail.

.Net Framework

The "*.Net Framework*" is a framework which provides you with a platform for writing the following kinds of applications:

- Web services
- Windows applications
- Web applications

Applications which are based on this framework can run on a variety of platforms. It is also possible for programmers to use the framework if they are programming in the following languages: C#, Javascript, VisualBasic, C++ and COBOL among others. The languages can also communicate with each other.

The framework provides a number of libraries that contain code which is used by these programming languages. Some of the components making up the framework include LINQ, Common Language Specification, Metadata and Assemblies, Windows Forms, ADO.Net,), Common Type System, Windows Presentation Foundation, Windows Workflow Foundation (WF), Windows Communication Foundation (WCF), ASP.Net and ASP.Net AJAX.

C# IDE (Integrated Development Environment)

To program in C#, you can use any of the following IDEs:

- Visual Web Developer
- Visual C#
- Visual Studio

You can use any of the above IDEs to write your C# programs, ranging from the simple to the complex ones. It is also possible for you to write the code in basic text editors like notepad and then execute the code via the command prompt. In this tutorial, we have used visual studio 2013 and the version of the ".Net Framework" installed on the machine is version 4.5. You can get these online and then download and install them on your computer. To install the "Express" version of visual studio 2013, make sure that you have an active internet connection.

For Linux and Mac OSX users

Unfortunately the *".Net Framework"* runs only on the Windows operating system. However, there exist alternatives which can be used on other types of operating systems. A good example of this is *"Mono"*. This version of *".Net Framework"* runs on a variety of operating systems including some of the versions of Linux and Mac OSX. It is open-source software, meaning that you can download, install and use it for free and it comes with a C# compiler as part of the installation.

Most people think *"Mono"* was developed for the purpose of providing the *".Net Framework"* for other versions of operating systems, rather than Linux. However, this software also provides Linux users with powerful tools for development purposes. Other operating systems on which *"Mono"* can run includes android, BSD, Solaris, iOS and Unix.

Chapter 3 - Structure of the program

Before getting into the actual C# programming, you need to understand the elements which will make up your programs. The following are the parts of a C# program:

- Namespace Declaration

- Comments

- Class methods

- A Class

- Class attributes

- Statements and Expressions

- A Main Method

We will now create our first program in C#. Just open the IDE and then write the following code:

using System;

namespace FirstProgram

```csharp
{
class Hello
{
static void Main(string[] args)
{
/* our first program in C# */
Console.WriteLine("Hello there");
Console.ReadKey();
}
}
}
```

Once you have written the program in the IDE, just click on the *"Run"* button at the top. You will observe the following output from the program:

```
Hello there
```

The first line of the code uses the keyword *"using"* and this is responsible for including *"System"* namespace into the program. In the second line of the code, we have declared the *"namespace"*, which is just a collection of classes. In the next line of code, we have declared our class and given it the name *"FirstProgram"*.

Notice that we have used the *"class"* keyword for us to declare the class. The next line of code specifies the main method for the class. When the class is executed, this method will determine what will happen. The next line of code forms the comment in the program. The compiler will not execute this but once it gets to it, it will skip it. The main method has then specified its behavior in the next line of code. This is the line *"Console.WriteLine("Hello World");"*. The last line of the code makes the program to wait for a key to be pressed.

It is good for you to note the following key points before getting deeper into the programming:

- All statements in C# must end with a semicolon (;)

- The language is case sensitive

- The program can take a different name to that of the class

- The execution of the program starts from the main method

Chapter 4 - C# Data Types

There are three kinds of variables in C#. These include the following:

- Value types
- Reference types
- Pointer types

Value Type Variables

These types of variables can be directly assigned a value. They are used after deriving them from the class "*System.ValueType*". The variable directly contains data. They include "*int*", "*long*" and "*char*", these are used for storage of integers, floating point numbers and characters respectively. Whenever you declare any of the above types, the computer will automatically reserve memory space for the variable.

Other value data types in C# include decimal, bool, byte, double, sbyte, ulong, ufloat, short and uint.

The method *"sizeof"* is used when the programmer wants to know the size of a particular variable under a certain circumstance. Use of the expression *"sizeof(type)"* will give the size of the storage of the type or object in question. Let us demonstrate this by use of an example:

```
using System;
namespace DataTypeApplication
{
class MyProgram
{
static void Main(string[] args)
{
Console.WriteLine("The size of the int: {0}", sizeof(int));
Console.ReadLine();
}
}
}
```

Write the program as it is above and then run it. You should get the following output:

```
The size of the int: 4
```

The result shows that 4 bytes are reserved for storage of the integer.

Reference Data Types

These do not hold the actual data of the variable instead they reference to that variable. To explain in other words, they point to the memory location of the variable. Multiple variables can reference to a location in the memory. In the case that a single variable changes the value of the variable which is already stored in the memory, then the other variables will reflect this automatically. Examples of these types of variables include the string, dynamic and object.

Object Data Type

This forms the base class for all types of data in C# CTS (Common Type System). It is an alias for the *"System.Object"* class. One of the good things of this type of data is that it can be assigned a value which belongs to the other data types such as reference and value types.

Boxing means that a value has been converted from value type to the object type. An example of this is given below:

object objct;

objct = 50; // this is called boxing

Dynamic Data Type

Any type of value can be stored in this type of data. Once you have stored the data it will be type-checked during the execution or run-time.

Declaration of a dynamic data type takes the following syntax:

dynamic <variable_name> = value;

Let us give an example of this:

dynamic data = 40;

You should have realized that dynamic data types are closely related to the object data types. The difference comes in type-checking of the values for the variables. In dynamic data type this occurs during the run-time whilst in the object data type it occurs during the compile time.

String Data Type

This data type allows programmers to assign string values to a variable. It is an alias for the class _"System.Class"_. The string type has been derived from the object data type. To assign a value to a string variable, we can use either the _"quoted"_ or the _"@quoted"_ method.

Consider the example given below:

String s = "Hello there";

The above example makes use of the _"quoted"_ method. Let us give an example of the other method, the _"@quoted"_ method:

@"Hello there";

Reference types which are user-defined include the interface, class or the delegate. You will learn how to use these in the next chapters.

The Pointer Data Type

This type of data is used to store the memory address of another data type. If you are well versed in C and C++, then you will have no problem with this type of data as this works the same in C# as in those two programming languages. Declaration of pointers takes the following syntax:

type* identifier;

Consider the example given below:

char* pointer;
int* ipointer;

Chapter 5 - Type Conversion in C#

In this case, one type of data is converted to another type. It is also referred to as *"type casting"*. There are two methods of type conversion. They are the following:

- Implicit type conversion- this is done in C# so as to ensure safety. It includes conversions from smaller to large integral values and conversion from derived classes to base classes.

- Explicit type conversion- in this case, users use functions which they define on their own so as to convert one type of data to another in an explicit manner. A cast operator is needed for this operation to take place.

Consider the example shown below:

```
using System;
namespace TypeCastingExample
{
Class Explicit
{
static void Main(string[] args)
{
double data = 500.45;
int j;
// type cast the above double value to an int.
j = (int)data;
Console.WriteLine(j);
Console.ReadKey();
}
}
}
```

The above example shows how explicit type conversion takes place. Run the program and then observe the result. It should be as follows:

$$500$$

As shown in the above figure, the double value has been converted to an integer value. This is explicit type conversion.

The following are some of the methods which are used in type conversion:

- **ToBoolean** – The specified type is converted to a Boolean if it is possible

- **ToChar** – The specified value is converted to a Unicode character if it is possible

- **ToByte** – The specified data is converted to a byte

- **ToDecimal** – A floating point value is converted to a float or a decimal type

- **ToDateTime** – A value of type integer or string is converted to a structure in form of a date or time

- **ToString** – The specified type is converted into a string

- **ToInt16** – The specified type is converted to a 16-bit integer

Consider the following example:

```
using System;
namespace TypeCastingExample
{
class StringCasting
{
static void Main(string[] args)
{
int j = 90;
float flt = 67.007f;
double data = 3345.8907;
bool bl = true;
Console.WriteLine(j.ToString());
Console.WriteLine(flt.ToString());
Console.WriteLine(data.ToString());
Console.WriteLine(bl.ToString());
Console.ReadKey();
}
}
}
```

Write the program as it is and then run it. The observed output will be as follows:

```
90
67.007
3345.8907
True
```

Chapter 6 - Variables in C#

A variable is a name representing a storage location. Notice that we can use the program to manipulate this storage area. A variable in C# must be given a type, and this will determine the amount of memory space that is reserved for the variable. It also determines the set of operations which can be applied to the value and the range of values that can be accepted for storage in that location.

The basic types in C# include the following:

- Integral types - ulong, short, byte, int, ushort, uint, long, sbyte, and char
- Floating point types - float and double
- Boolean types - true or false values, as assigned
- Decimal types - decimal
- Nullable types - Nullable data types

With C#, you can also define other types of values such as "*enum*" (enumerators) and "*class*" which is a reference type. To declare a variable in C#, we use the following syntax:

<data_type> <variable_list>;

The "*data_type*" can be any type as long as it a valid type in C#. The "*variable_list*" can only be made up of a single variable or multiple variables separated by use of a comma.

The following examples shows how we can declare variables in C#:

int a, b, c;

char d, ch;

float f, height;

double d;

Variable initialization can be done at the same time with variable declaration. This is shown in the example below:

int j = 12;

Initialization of variables

To assign a value to a variable, we use an equal sign. This should then be followed by the constant expression. It takes the following syntax:

variable_name = value;

Consider the following examples about variable declaration in C#:

int b = 4, c = 10;   /* initializing b and c. */

byte y = 24;   /* initializing y. */

double salary = 424.78986; /* initializing salary as a double */

char male = 'm';   /* initializing the value of male as "m" */

If you initialize variables in the wrong manner, then your program might produce an error. An example is when you initialize a wrong value for the variable.

Consider the following example which uses various types of variables:

```
using System;
namespace Variables
{
class MyProgram
{
static void Main(string[] args)
{
short x;
int y ;
double p;

/* actual initialization */
x = 30;
y = 90;
p = x + y;
Console.WriteLine("x = {0}, y = {1}, p = {2}", x, y, p);
Console.ReadLine();
```

```
}

}

}
```

Write the program as it is and the run it. You will observe the following output:

$$x = 30, \; y = 90, \; p = 120$$

We have printed the values for the variables as well as their sum.

Chapter 7 - Decision Making in C#

C# supports the use of decision making statements. The program defines or specifies a set of conditions for the program. Statements, which are the actions to be taken or executed when each of the condition is met, are also specified. The program should also specify the set of statements which should be executed if the condition is not met.

We will discuss the several decision making statements which are supported in C#.

"if" Statement

This is made up of a Boolean expression which is then followed by the statement or the set of statements. The statement takes the following syntax:

if(boolean_expression)

{

/* statement(s) to be executed if the above expression

is met*/

}

If the specified Boolean expression is found to be true, then the statement(s) placed inside the block will be executed. If this is not the case, that is, the Boolean expression is found to be false, then the set of statement(s) after the curly bracket will be executed.

Consider the following example:

using System;

namespace IfStatement

{

```
class MyProgram
{
static void Main(string[] args)
{
/* defining our local variable */
int x = 20;
/* using the "if" statement to check the Boolean
condition */
if (x < 50)
{
/* if the expression is true, the following statement
will be executed */
Console.WriteLine("x is less than 50");
}
Console.WriteLine("The value of x is : {0}", x);
Console.ReadLine();
}
}
```

Write the program as it is and then run it. You will get the following as the output:

```
x is less than 50
The value of x is : 20
```

The Boolean expression was met and that is why we get the output as the statement under it. Suppose that the condition was not met?

```csharp
using System;

namespace IfStatement
{
class MyProgram
{
static void Main(string[] args)
{
/* defining our local variable */
int x = 90;
/* using the "if" statement to check the Boolean
condition */
if (x < 50)
{
/* if the expression is true, the following statement
will be executed */
Console.WriteLine("x is less than 50");
}
Console.WriteLine("The value of x is : {0}", x);
Console.ReadLine();
}
```

```
}

}
```

Execute the above program and then observe the output from it. It will be as follows:

```
The value of x is : 90
```

The reason for the above output is that the Boolean expression was not met. The program then executed the alternative statement.

"if...else" statement

This is used for a more effective execution of the condition. The "*if*" statement in this case is followed by an "*else*" statement. This is executed if the Boolean expression is found to be false.

It takes the following syntax:

if(boolean_expression)

{

/* statement(s) to be executed if the condition is met

***/**

}

else

{

/* statement(s) to be executed if the condition is not

met*/

}

We will now demonstrate this by use of an example. Consider the one given below:

```
using System;
namespace IfElseStatement
{
class MyProgram
{
static void Main(string[] args)
{
/* defining our local variable */
int x = 90;


/* checking by use of a Boolean expression */
if (x < 50)
{
/* if the condition is met, then the following
statement will be executed */
Console.WriteLine("x is less than 50");
}
```

else

{

/* the following statement will be executed if

condition is not met */

Console.WriteLine("x is greater than 50");

}

Console.WriteLine("The value of x is : {0}", x);

Console.ReadLine();

}

}

}

Write the program as it is and then run it. You will get the following result as the output:

```
x is greater than 50
The value of x is : 90
```

The last statements, that is those which are under the *"else"* statement, have been executed. The reason is because our Boolean expression was not met.

Suppose the condition was met by initializing the variable "*x*" to a value which is less than 50, we would get the following result:

```
x is less than 50
The value of x is : 40
```

The output shown in the above figure shows that the value of variable "*x*" is 40.

"if...else if...else" Statement

The "*if*" statement can have an "*else if...else*" statement which is optional for testing of the various conditions which might be present in our program. The statement takes the following syntax:

if(boolean_expression a)

{

/* this will execute if the above Boolean expression is met */

}

else if(boolean_expression b)

{

/* this will execute if Boolean expression "*b*" is met */

}

else if(boolean_expression c)

{

/* this will execute if Boolean expression "*c*" is met */

}

else

```csharp
{
/* this will be executed if none of the conditions is met
*/
}
```

Let us demonstrate this by use of an example:

```csharp
using System;
namespace OurStatement
{
class MyProgram
{
static void Main(string[] args)
{
/* defining our local variable */
int x = 90;
/* check the boolean condition */
if (x == 20)
{
/* if the condition is met, the statement below will be
executed */
```

```
Console.WriteLine("The Value of x is 20");
}
else if (x == 40)
{
/* checking the condition*/
Console.WriteLine("The Value of x is 40");
}
else if (x == 60)
{
/* checking whether condition is true*/
Console.WriteLine("The Value of x is 60");
}
else
{
/* this will be executed if no condition was met*/
Console.WriteLine("No value was matched");
}
Console.WriteLine("The Exact value of x is: {0}", x);
Console.ReadLine();
}
```

```
}

}
```

Write the program and then run it.

You will observe the following output:

```
No value was matched
The Exact value of x is: 90
```

The above figure shows that no value was met. Suppose that we set the value of "*x*" to be 40, then the program will give use the following output:

```
The Value of x is 40
The Exact value of x is: 40
```

The output shows that all the conditions in the program are executable, thus, our statement works efficiently.

Nested "if" Statements

The "*if*" or "*else if*" statements can be nested, meaning that they can be placed inside another "*if*" or "*else if*" statement.

Nested "*if*" statement takes the following syntax:

if(boolean_expression a)

{

/* this will be executed if Boolean expression a is met*/

if(boolean_expression b)

{

/* this will be executed if Boolean expression b is met

*/

}

}

To nest the "*else if...else*" statement, use the same syntax as above.

Consider the following example:

```
using System;

namespace DecisonStatement

{

class MyProgram

{

static void Main(string[] args)

{

//* defining our local variable */

int x = 90;

int y = 150;


/* the Boolean condition */

if (x == 90)

{

/* the statement will be executed if the above

condition is met */

if (y == 150)
```

```
{
/* this will be executed if the condition is met */
Console.WriteLine("The Value of x is 90 and y is
150");
}
}
Console.WriteLine("The Exact value of x is : {0}", x);
Console.WriteLine("The Exact value of y is : {0}", y);
Console.ReadLine();
}
}
}
```

Write the program, save it and then run it. Observe the resulting output which should be as follows:

```
The Value of x is 90 and y is 150
The Exact value of x is : 90
The Exact value of y is : 150
```

The "switch" statement

With this statement, the programmer can test whether the value of a variable is equal to some other values. In this case, the values are the "*case*". The statement takes the following syntax:

```
switch(expression) {

case constant-condition  :

statement(s);

break;

case constant-condition  :

statement(s);

break;

/* you can continue with the "case" statements */

default : statement(s);

}
```

Let us demonstrate this by the following example:

```
using System;
namespace DecisionStatement
{
class MyProgram
{
static void Main(string[] args)
{
/* defining our local variable */
char letter = 'A';
switch (letter)
{
case 'A':
Console.WriteLine("A for Apple!");
break;
case 'B':
case 'C':
Console.WriteLine("B for boy and C for cow");
```

```
break;
case 'D':
Console.WriteLine("D for dog");
break;
case 'E':
Console.WriteLine("E for eagle");
break;
default:
Console.WriteLine("The letter is unknown");
break;
}
Console.WriteLine("The letter is {0}", letter);
Console.ReadLine();
}
}
}
```

Write the program as it is and the run it.

You will observe the following output:

```
A for Apple!
The letter is  A
```

The letter has been found. Suppose we change the letter to the one which is not defined. We will get the following result:

The letter is unknown
The letter is X

The output shows that I entered the letter "*X*" which is not defined in the program.

Nested "switch" statement

A "switch" statement can be placed inside another "switch" statement as a part of it. This takes the following syntax:

```
switch(c1)
{
case 'X':
printf("The X is part of the outer part of the switch" );
switch(c2)
{
case 'Y':
printf("The Y is part of the inner switch" );
break;
case 'Z': /* this is an inner Z */
}
break;
case 'Y': /* This is an outer Y */
}
```

Let us demonstrate this by use of an example. Open your IDE and then write the following program:

```
using System;
namespace DecisionStatement
{
class MyProgram
{
static void Main(string[] args)
{
int x = 90;
int y = 150;
switch (x)
{
case 90:
Console.WriteLine("This forms an outer switch ");
switch (y)
{
case 150:
Console.WriteLine("This forms an inner switch ");
```

```
break;

}

break;

}

Console.WriteLine("The exact value of x is : {0}", x);

Console.WriteLine("The exact value of y is : {0}", y);

Console.ReadLine();

}

}

}
```

Write the program as shown above. Save and then run it. You will observe the following as the output:

```
This forms an outer switch
This forms an inner switch
The exact value of x is : 90
The exact value of y is : 150
```

Chapter 8 - Loops in C#

Loops are mostly used when the programmer wants to specify the number of times that a section of code should be executed. The statements which are specified in a loop are executed in a sequential manner, meaning that the execution is done from the first statement to the second and so on. Let us discuss some of the loops supported in C#.

The "while" Loop

This loop will continue to execute the specified statement provided the set condition is met or is true. If it evaluates and then it finds that the condition is being violated, then it will immediately halt its execution. The loop takes the following syntax:

while(condition)

{

statement(s);

}

The loop can allow a single or multiple statements for execution. The statements which are below the loop will be executed if the condition under test becomes false. Notice that it is possible for the *"while"* loop to never execute.

Consider the example given below:

```
using System;
namespace Loop
{
class MyProgram
{
static void Main(string[] args)
{
/* defining the local variable */
int x = 20;
/* while loop execution */
while (x < 30)
{
Console.WriteLine("The value of x is: {0}", x);
x++;
```

```
}

Console.ReadLine();

}

}

}
```

Write the program as it is and then run it. You will observe the
following output:

```
The value of x is: 20
The value of x is: 21
The value of x is: 22
The value of x is: 23
The value of x is: 24
The value of x is: 25
The value of x is: 26
The value of x is: 27
The value of x is: 28
The value of x is: 29
```

The loop will execute as long as the value of variable "x" is less than 30. When the loop finds that the value of "x" is equals to 30, it will halt its execution as doing so will violate the condition. This explains why we have 29 as the last value of the variable. Notice that the value of the variable is incremented by 1 on each successful execution of the loop.

The "for" Loop

With this, you just specify the number of times that you need your loop to be executed. The loop takes the following syntax:

for (initialization; condition; increment/decrement)

{

statement(s);

}

The "*initialization*" is responsible for setting the initial value of the loop. The "*condition*" specifies the time at which the loop should be executed, while "*increment/decrement*" specifies how to increase or decrease the variable that counts the number of times that the loop has been executed.

After each execution of the loop, the condition is evaluated to determine if it is still being met or not. If the condition is found to be true, then the loop is executed. If it is found to be false, then the loop halts execution.

Let us demonstrate this by use of an example:

```csharp
using System;
namespace Loop
{
class MyProgram
{
static void Main(string[] args)
{
/* execution of the "for" loop */
for (int x = 0; x < 10; x = x + 1)
{
Console.WriteLine("The value of x is: {0}", x);
}
Console.ReadLine();
}
}
}
```

Write the program as it is and then execute it. You will observe the following output:

```
The value of x is: 0
The value of x is: 1
The value of x is: 2
The value of x is: 3
The value of x is: 4
The value of x is: 5
The value of x is: 6
The value of x is: 7
The value of x is: 8
The value of x is: 9
```

We specified that the value of the variable "x" should be less than 10. You can see that the loop has executed until it has found that it is violating the condition. This is why we do not have value 10 in the output.

The "Do...While" Loop

This loop works in contrast to how the other loops work. The condition is checked at the end of the loop. For the case of the *"while"* and the *"for"* loop, the condition is checked at the start of loop.

This loop works in the same way as the *"while"* loop. However, we said that the latter can never execute, if the condition is found to be false. For the case of the former, we are guaranteed of at least a single execution of the loop. The loop takes the following syntax:

do

{

statement(s);

}while(condition);

The condition expression has been placed at the end of the loop, meaning that the statements placed inside the loop will be executed once before the condition is evaluated. If it is found to be false, then it will have been executed once. If true, then the execution will continue.

Let us demonstrate the use of this loop by use of an example:

```
using System;

namespace Loop

{

    class MyProgram

{

static void Main(string[] args)

{

/* defining our local variable */

int x = 20;


/* executing the "do" loop */

do

{

Console.WriteLine("The value of x is: {0}", x);

x = x + 1;

}

while (x < 30);
```

Console.ReadLine();

}

}

}

Again, write the above program just as it is and then execute.
You will observe the following output:

```
The value of x is: 20
The value of x is: 21
The value of x is: 22
The value of x is: 23
The value of x is: 24
The value of x is: 25
The value of x is: 26
The value of x is: 27
The value of x is: 28
The value of x is: 29
```

The loop has executed since the value of the variable was found to be less than 30. The execution continued and on each successful execution of the loop, the value of the variable was incremented by 1. The value 30 for the variable has not been printed because this would violate the test condition. Suppose the test condition was not met, that is, setting the value of x to a value which is greater than 30, say 40. The result would be as follows:

```
The value of x is: 40
```

The loop has not been executed again as doing this would violate the test condition that is, that the value of the variable should be less than 30. Even though the test condition was violated, the loop has executed once. That is how this type of loop works.

Nested Loops

In C#, it is possible for us to place a loop inside another loop. These are called *"Nested Loops"*. Nested *"for"* loop take the following syntax in C#:

for (initialization; condition; increment/decrement)

{

for (initialization; condition; increment/decrement)

{

statement(s);

}

statement(s);

}

Nested *"while"* loop takes the following syntax in C#:

while(condition)

{

while(condition)

{

statement(s);

}

statement(s);

}

Nested *"do...while"* loop takes the following syntax:

```
do
{
statement(s);
do
{
statement(s);
}
while( condition );

}
while( condition );
```

You also need to note that it is possible for the programmer to use any loop inside another type of loop, for example, a *"while"* loop can be nested inside the *"for"* loop. The vice versa is also true.

Consider the example given below which shows how to nest a *"for"* loop:

```
using System;
namespace NestingLoops
{
class MyProgram
{
static void Main(string[] args)
{
/* defining our local variable */
int x, y;
for (x = 2; x < 100; x++)
{
for (y = 2; y <= (x / y); y++)
if ((x % y) == 0) break; // the number is not prime if a
factor is found
if (y > (x / y))
Console.WriteLine("{0} is a prime number", x);
}
```

Console.ReadLine();

}

}

}

In the program, we need to find prime numbers between 2 and 20. Write the program and then run it. You will observe the following output:

```
2 is a prime number
3 is a prime number
5 is a prime number
7 is a prime number
11 is a prime number
13 is a prime number
17 is a prime number
19 is a prime number
```

The nested loop has worked effectively since we have got the prime numbers.

Chapter 9 - Encapsulation in C#

With encapsulation, programmers can use a package for enclosing either one or more items within it. This feature is very interesting and was introduced by the object-oriented technology. It prevents the users of the program from accessing the implementation details of the program.

The feature is closely related to the concept of *"Abstraction"*. With abstraction, only the relevant issues are made visible and accessible to the users. The role of encapsulation is to enable the programmer to implement the concept of abstraction.

To implement encapsulation in a program, we make use of *"access specifiers"*. With access specifiers, the programmer will be in a position to specify how visible a class member is. The following access specifiers are supported in C#:

- Protected internal
- Private
- Public
- Protected
- Internal

Public Acces Specifier

With this type of access specifier, the programmer is able to expose the member variables and member functions that they define to the other functions and variables. It is possible to access them outside the class in which they are defined. Let us demonstrate this by use of an example:

```
using System;
namespace PublicAccessSpecifier
{
class MyRectangle
{
//defining member variables
public double width;
public double length;
public double CalculateArea()
{
Return width * length;
}
public void ShowArea()
```

```csharp
{
Console.WriteLine("The Width is: {0}", width);
Console.WriteLine("The Length is: {0}", length);
Console.WriteLine("The Area is: {0}",
CalculateArea());
}
}//ending the class MyRectangle
class RunRectangle
{
static void Main(string[] args)
{
MyRectangle rec = new MyRectangle();
rec.width = 1.5;
rec.length = 3.5;
rec.ShowArea();
Console.ReadLine();
}
}
}
```

Write the above program and then run it. You will notice the following output:

```
The Width is: 1.5
The Length is: 3.5
The Area is: 5.25
```

We have made the member variables publicly accessible by use of the keyword "*public*". We have then created an instance of the class "*MyRectangle*" and given it the name "*rec*". This instance has been used to access the member variables.

Private Access Specifier

With the private access specifier, the programmer hides the member functions and the member functions of a class from other functions and variables. Functions of the same class are the only ones which will be able to access the variables. Notice that in this case, instantiation of the class is not needed because the instance will not be able to access the private functions and variables.

Consider the example given below:

```
using System;
namespace PrivateAccessSpecifiers
{
class MyRectangle
{
//defining the member
private double width;
private double length;
public void GetRecDetails()
{
```

```csharp
Console.WriteLine("Please enter the width: ");

width = Convert.ToDouble(Console.ReadLine());

Console.WriteLine("Please enter the length: ");

length = Convert.ToDouble(Console.ReadLine());

}

public double CalculateArea()

{

return  width * length;

}

public void ShowArea()

{

Console.WriteLine("The Width is: {0}", width);

Console.WriteLine("The Length is: {0}", length);

Console.WriteLine("The Area is: {0}",

CalculateArea());

}

}//ending our class

class ExecuteClass

{

static void Main(string[] args)
```

```
{
MyRectangle rec = new MyRectangle();
rec.GetRecDetails();
rec.ShowArea();
Console.ReadLine();
}
}
}
```

Write the program and then execute it. You will be prompted to provide both the length and the width of the rectangle. The console for this will be as follows:

```
Please enter the width:
```

Just provide the width in the above console and then press the "*Enter*" key. You will see the console for providing the length. It will be as follows:

```
Please enter the Length:
```

Just provide the length and then hit the "*Enter*" key. You will be provided with the area. In my case, the length was 3.5 and the width was 1.5. I then got the following:

```
The Area is: 5.25
```

Internal Access Specifier

With this, the class is made to expose its member functions and member variables to the other objects and functions currently in the assembly. To make it clear, any variable or function defined with an internal access specifier can be accessed from any other class which is within the application where these have been defined.

Consider the example given below:

```
using System;
namespace AccessSpecifier
{
class MyRectangle
{
//defining the member variables
internal double width;
internal double length;
double CalculateArea()
{
return width * length;
```

```
}
public void ShowArea()
{
Console.WriteLine("The Width is: {0}", width);
Console.WriteLine("The Length is: {0}", length);
Console.WriteLine("The Area is: {0}",
CalculateArea());
}
}//Ending our class
class RunRectangle
{
static void Main(string[] args)
{
MyRectangle rec = new MyRectangle();
rec.width = 1.5;
rec.length = 3.5;
rec.ShowArea();
Console.ReadLine();
}
}
```

```
}
```

Just write the program the way it is and then run or execute it. The following output will be observed:

```
The Width is: 1.5
The Length is: 3.5
The Area is: 5.25
```

As shown in the above figure, our access specifier has worked effectively.

Chapter 10 - Methods in C#

A method is made up of a group of statements which are grouped for the sake of performing a particular task. In C# nearly every class has the main method. To use a method in C#, you have defined and then call it.

How to define Methods in C#

Defining a method means that you declare the elements which make up its structure. This takes the following syntax:

<Access Specifier> <Return Type>

<Name>(Arguments List)

{

Body

}

The "*Access Specifier*" will determine how the method is accessible from the other methods and functions from the same or different class.

If a method is expected to return a value, then the "*Return Type*" will specify the type of data which is being returned. However, for methods which are not expected to return any value, then this is declared to be "*void*".

The "*Name*" specifies the name of your method. Note that this should be unique, so do not give the method a name which has already been used in the same class for identifying another entity.

The "*Argument List*" specifies the parameters to be used for passing of data, note that you can specify any number of parameters. You should also specify their data type. However, some methods take no parameters.

The "*Body*" is the rest of the activities to be accomplished in the class.

Consider the example shown below:

```
class Number
{
public int CheckMax(int number1, int number2)
{
/* declaring our local variable */
int answer;
if (number1 > number2)
answer = number1;
else
answer = number2;
return answer;
}
...
}
```

n the above method, we are passing our two parameters which are of integer data type. Our intention is to find the maximum between the two numbers.

How to call methods in C#

In C#, methods are called by their names. Consider the following example:

```
using System;

        namespace MethodApp
{
class NumMan
{
public int CheckMax(int number1, int number2)
{
/* declaring our local variable */
int answer;
if (number1 > number2)
answer = number1;
```

```csharp
else
answer = number2;
return answer;
}
static void Main(string[] args)
{
/* dfining the local variable */
int x = 90;
int y = 150;
int r;
NumMan nm = new NumMan ();
//calling the CheckMax method
r = nm.CheckMax(x, y);
Console.WriteLine("The Maximum value is : {0}", r );
Console.ReadLine();
}
}
}
```

Write the program and then run it. Observe the result which will be as follows:

```
The Maximum value is : 150
```

The method was intended to check for the maximum number between the two values for the variables. From the figure above, it is very clear that the method has worked effectively since 150 is greater than 90. You now know how to call methods in C#.

If the method is publicly accessible, then it is possible for us to call it by use of the instance of the method. In our case, the method is named *"CheckMax()"* and belongs to the class *"NumMan"*. It is possible for us to call the method from outside this class.

This is demonstrated below:

```
using System;
namespace MthodApp
{
class NumMan
{
public int CheckMax(int number1, int number2)
{
/* declaring our local variable */
int answer;
if(number1 > number2)
answer = number1;
else
answer = number2;
return answer;
}
}
class T
```

```
{
static void Main(string[] args)
{
/* defining our local variable */
int x = 90;
int y = 150;
int r;
NumMan nm = new NumMan ();
//calling the CheckMax method
r = nm.CheckMax(x, y);
Console.WriteLine("The Maximum value is : {0}", r );
Console.ReadLine();
}
}
}
```

Write the program as shown above and then execute or run it.
Observe the output, which should be as follows:

```
The Maximum value is : 150
```

Calling a method Recursively

This means a method calling itself. The following example program shows how this happens by use of a recursive function so as to calculate the factorial of the number.

```
using System;
namespace MethodApp
{
class NumMan
{
public int factorial(int number)
{
/* declaring our local variable */
int answer;
if (number == 1)
{
return 1;
}
else
{
```

```
answer = factorial(number - 1) * number;

return answer;

}

}

static void Main(string[] args)

{

NumMan nm = new NumMan ();

//calling the method, that is "factorial"

Console.WriteLine("The factorial of 8 is : {0}",

nm.factorial(8));

Console.WriteLine("The factorial of 9 is : {0}",

nm.factorial(9));

Console.WriteLine("The factorial of 10 is : {0}",

nm.factorial(10));

Console.ReadLine();

}

}

}
```

Just write the program as it is shown and then execute it. You will observe the following as the output from the program:

```
The factorial of 8 is : 40320
The factorial of 9 is : 362880
The factorial of 10 is : 3628800
```

We have specified the formula for calculating the factorial of a number. To call the method "*factorial*", we have just used its name. This is what we call "*recursion*".

Chapter 11 - Classes in C#

A class represents a blueprint for a data type. From the class definition, we can tell the object which makes it and the kind of operations which can be performed on these objects. The objects in this case are instances of the class. The members of a class are the variables and the methods which make it.

Class Definition

To define a class, we being by the keyword *"class"* which is followed by the name of the class. The body of the class is enclosed with curly braces.

The following shows the syntax for the same:

```
<access specifier> class  name
{
// the member variables
<access specifier> <data type> variable_a;
<access specifier> <data type> variable_b;
...
<access specifier> <data type> variable_n;
// the member methods
<access specifier> <return type>
method_a(parameter_list)
{
// the method body
}
<access specifier> <return type>
method_b(parameter_list)
{
// the method body
}
```

...

<access specifier> <return type>

method_n(parameter_list)

{

// the method body

}

}

With the "*access specifiers*" we will be able to define which of the members of the class, as well as the class itself are, accessible. By default, the access level for the members is "*private*".

The "*data type*" will specify the type of data that the variables of the class will take.

The "*return type*" will specify the type of data that we expect to get back from the methods. The dot (.) operator is used for accessing the members of the class.

Let us illustrate this by use of an example:

```
using System;
namespace Class App
{
class MyBox
{
public double breadth;  // the breadth of our box
public double length;   // the length of our box
public double height;   // the height of our box
}
class Tester
{
static void Main(string[] args)
{
MyBox B1 = new MyBox();   //instantiation of the class to get object B1

MyBox B2 = new MyBox();   // instantiation of the class to get object B2

double volume = 0.0;   // this will store the volume of our box
```

```csharp
// specifications for box 1

Box1.breadth = 5.0;

B1.length = 9.0;

B1.height = 8.0;

// specifications for box 2

B2.breadth = 15.0;

B2.length = 11.0;

B2.height = 9.0;

// volume for the B1 1

volume = B1.breadth * B1.length * B1.height;

Console.WriteLine("The volume for B1 is : {0}",
volume);


// volume for B 2

volume = B2.breadth * B2.length * B2.height;

Console.WriteLine("The volume for B2 is: {0}",
volume);
Console.ReadKey();

}

}

}
```

What the class does is to calculate the volume of the boxes for you. To calculate the volume, we must specify the breadth, the height and the length of the box which is cuboid in shape. These are then multiplied together and the result is the volume. Write the program as it is and then execute. Observe the output that you get from it.

Conclusion

It can be concluded that C# is a very powerful programming which can be used for the development of amazing apps. For users who have knowledge C and C++ programming, it is usually easy to learn this language as most constructs are closely related in these programming languages. The language supports multiple programming paradigms, including imperative, functional and the famous and powerful object-oriented programming paradigm.

The language is part of the *".Net Framework"* which was written by Microsoft. This means that the framework must be installed on your system before starting the act of programming in C#. Once you have installed the framework, you need to install the IDE, which is the *"Microsoft Visual Studio"*. It is after this that you can get stated.

The language has a number of features which have been discussed in this book, hopefully you are now familiar with these features. For instance, the programming language supports a wide variety of data types, including the user-defined ones. This shows that the programmer has some freedom. The language also supports *"type conversion"*, whereby one type of data is converted to another type of data.

Notice that all statements in C# end with a semicolon (;), so if you leave this out, you will get an error in your program. Since the programming language is object-oriented, it has strong support for object-oriented programming features. It is possible for programmers to define classes in C# and then instantiate them.

The language also supports the use of access specifiers so as to define the level of accessibility of the member functions and variables of a particular program. It is also possible for one to define methods in C# and then pass any number of parameters to them. Decision making statements are highly supported in C# as well as loops. It is also possible to nest the loops in C#.

Thank you!

We would like to thank you for buying this book. Hope you found it helpful in your trip to BECOME AN EXPERT in programming field. And we are happy to recommend you some other books from this author:

1. JAVA 8 PROGRAMMING: Step by Step Java 8 Course Programming (BECOME AN EXPERT Book 1)

http://www.amazon.com/gp/product/B012BDR 7CC?*Version*=1&*entries*=0

2. ASP.NET MVC 5: Learn ASP.net MTV 5 Programming

FAST and EASY (From Zero to Professional 1)

http://www.amazon.com/gp/product/B014FV25T8?*Version*=1&*entries*=0

3. AngularJS: Master AngularJS with Simple Steps and Instructions (From Zero to Professional Book 2)

http://www.amazon.com/gp/product/B016W FXOI6?*Version*=1&*entries*=0